Stop Talking &

Start *Writing*

Your Book

Terrance Zepke

Stop Talking &

Start *Writing*

Your Book

Terrance Zepke

Safari Publishing

Copyright © 2015 by Terrance Zepke

Safari Publishing

All queries should be directed to www.safaripublishing.net

Library of Congress Cataloging-in-Publication Data

Zepke, Terrance

Stop Talking & Start Writing Your Book/Terrance Zepke p. cm.

ISBN: 9780990765332

1. Writing. 2. Writing Tips. 3. How to Write a Book. 4. Publishing. 5. Fiction-Writing. 6. Nonfiction-Writing. 7. Indie Publishing. 8. Language Arts-Publishing. 9. Writing Guide. I. Title.

First edition

10 9 8 7 6 5 4 3 2 1

Cover design by Sara Whitford

Foreword by Sara Whitford

When I first met Terrance Zepke back in 2001, she was already an established author with an impressive catalog of books. Being a highly creative individual, as well as a prolific writer, since that time she has more than tripled her list of available titles. Years ago, I confessed to her that I had been working on a novel of my own for quite some time, but I never seemed to be able to finish it. Every now and then, Terrance would ask me how my writing was coming along. I'd give her updates, which looking back on it probably made her think I would never finish the thing. Still, being a good friend, she would patiently offer words of encouragement and tell me I needed to stop worrying about everything being perfect and just finish the first draft. I'd say, "I know." But the truth is, I had worked on that manuscript for so long, and I had convinced myself that I couldn't consider the draft finished unless it was "just right."

Eventually, I threw up my hands in surrender and decided it was time for a fresh start. In May 2014, I ditched the half-completed manuscript that I had been working at on and off for seven long years and started on something new. This time I made a detailed outline to ensure I knew where the story was going.

When I told Terrance what I had done—

abandoning my previous project and starting a brand new one—I could virtually hear the look of consternation on her face over the phone. I told her I was determined to finish this time and letting go of that earlier project was just what I needed to do to get the creativity flowing again. I could tell she was both worried and skeptical. She had heard me go on and on about the previous project for years, and yet now I was going to hit the reset button and start all over again? Then she told me something that made me more determined than ever to complete a novel this time. She said, "You'll never finish if you don't stop being a perfectionist and stop talking about it. Just get the first draft written!"

I had already decided that was what I needed to do, but hearing her say the words made me even more determined to prove to myself that I could do it. And you know what? I did do it. Less than ten months after I started working on it, my novel was published and being enjoyed by readers around the globe. And now—just a little more than a year later—I'm weeks away from releasing book two of that series.

When Terrance says *Stop Talking & Start Writing Your Book*, she means it, and she has a whole slew of strategies to help you get the job done.

Sara Whitford is the author of the popular Adam Fletcher Adventure Series: *Smuggler's Gambit* and *Captured in the Caribbean.*

Introduction

Have you been talking about writing a book longer than you care to remember? When are you going to stop talking and start writing? I can help you make your dream a reality.

I'm going to let you in on a little secret. Even though I have written twenty-eight books, post a weekly *A Writer's Journey* blog, and co-host *A* **Writer's Journey: From Blank Page to Published**, I had no intention of writing a book about writing. What made me do it was seeing so many books on the market about how to write a book in a weekend or ten or thirty or sixty days. The final straw was when I saw a book for sale promising those naïve enough to believe it that they could write a book in **twenty-four hours**!

I'm going to be honest. These promises really get to me. I know you can't do it in a day or even thirty days, so I was curious as to who these authors were and exactly how they were going to make good on their promises. After doing a bit of research, I discovered that most of these people were not even writers! Most had no writing credentials other than a self-published e-book or two about writing. Now I'm not saying that you have to be a best-selling author to dispense writing advice, but I do take issue with someone who has little or no experience instructing others. Do you want a real doctor who has graduated from medical school in the operating room performing your surgery or some guy who has never been to med school but thinks he knows as much as a doctor?

Furthermore, I didn't like their advice because I knew it wouldn't work, and it really got to me that folks who don't know a thing about writing or the publishing industry are saying they can help you achieve this lofty goal so quickly and easily.

Do you really believe it's possible to write a book in twenty-four hours or over the weekend or in ten days? I guess folks really want to believe it's that simple. Well, here's a news bulletin. It takes a lot to get from an idea to writing the last sentence of a book. And these folks aren't going to get you there. When I read the descriptions and samples of some of these so-called writing books, the advice was ridiculous. One actually claimed that *"You don't have to be a good writer. You don't have to have a book idea. You don't have to have much time. You don't even have to like to write."*

Whoa! I'll tell you up front that no book worth reading was written in a day or by someone who was a bad writer. I also promise you that *this* book will truly be a valuable resource. I have included everything I know from years of writing workshops, writing courses, and personal experience. As I said, I don't promise you can do this in a day or that it will be easy. Writing is hard work. I'm not going to lie. Publishing is tough. No lie. And selling your book is beyond hard work. It is despairingly difficult! But it can be done if you go about it the right way.

Truth #1: I can (and will) show you how to write a book. I've been in this business a long time. I know what you have to do to be successful. I have been making a living as a writer for seventeen years. I am an award-winning author of twenty-eight books. All of my titles are *still* in print and *still* selling well. Seven of my books are in their ninth or tenth printing. Three of my books have been Amazon bestsellers. I am a hybrid author, meaning I am traditionally published and have done some indie publishing too. I write fiction, nonfiction, and creative nonfiction so I understand the needs and challenges of all writers. I have learned many things the hard way and hope to spare you those mistakes. Much of my knowledge is the result of being in this industry for so many years. I know the writing, publishing, and bookselling industry quite well.

Truth #2: It will require a great deal of you. We're talking blood, sweat, and tears. (Spoiler Alert: No blood will actually be shed, but there will probably be lots of sweat and a few tears along the way.) You should write because you are driven. You love to write. You need to write. You want to write. You have something to say. You should not write a book just because you want to be famous or get rich or think it's an easy way to make a living. Trust me, it's not! But it is a very rewarding career if you're going into it for the right reasons.

Truth #3: It cannot be done in a few hours or even a few days. Know up front that this is not going to be quick or easy. Are you *really* serious about this? Do you *really* want to do this? As with anything creative, you must be all in. You cannot make a half-hearted effort. If you are serious and really want this, then the good news is that you can do it and what you create will be something you can be proud of and that will sell—if you follow my advice. What's more, it will be the cornerstone of your long-lasting writing career. Yes! You will be building something real and long-lasting if you do it right. As I mentioned earlier, I have written fiction, nonfiction, and creative nonfiction, so I know the complexities and creative process (and challenges) for all types of writing.

This book focuses exclusively on the writing process. Throughout this reference you'll learn exactly what you need to know to write a book and the pitfalls to avoid, such as the three acts, how to develop your protagonist, how to beat writer's block, how to avoid the middle lull, and much more. There is even a step-by-step guide at the back of the book that will show you how to take what you have learned from this book and put it into practice.

Once you have written your book, be sure to get the next book in this series, which addresses the publishing process, *Stop Talking & Start Publishing Your Book*. The third book in this series is all about selling your book once you have written and published it, *Stop Talking & Start Selling Your Book*. If you stick with this series, I will navigate you through the tricky and often tedious process of writing, publishing, and selling your book. While I cannot guarantee you will become a best-selling novelist, I can guarantee that I am giving you the best information and advice.

If you want to know more about me or my titles, learn more about my blogs, podcasts, or subscribe to my weekly newsletter visit www.terrancezepke.com and www.terrancetalkstravel.com.

Here's the best advice you'll ever get about writing:

Stop dreaming about it or pondering it or hoping to find time someday or talking about writing a book and just get on with it!

Listen and Learn!

Podcast is available on www.terrancezepke.com and www.sarawhitford.com.

You can also subscribe to this podcast at iTunes: https://itunes.apple.com/us/podcast/writers-journey-from-blank/id911131840

How to Use This Book

Since you have bought or borrowed this book, I'm making some assumptions that I hope are true:

1. You want to be a writer.
2. You have an idea for a book.
3. You understand that I can show you how to achieve your goal, but I cannot make you sit down and write or give you talent.
4. You are committed and plan to write consistently. You are willing to work hard and make sacrifices to achieve your goal.
5. You understand that this book focuses on the creative process. This means I will show you how to go from an idea to a finished book. I will not be discussing sentence structure and punctuation rules. I don't want you to even think about editing until you are done writing.

To best utilize this reference, be sure to read all chapters and check out the chapter summary at the conclusion of each chapter, as well as the *Bonus! Month by Month Guide to Writing a Book*, which is at the end of this reference.

Pledge Form

I, _____, do solemnly
promise to give this my best effort.

I vow to:

___Develop a daily writing routine.

_____Set writing goals.

_____I will not let distractions derail me.

_____I will seek help if I need it.

_____I will stay focused. If I hit the wall, I will get back
on track.

_____

(Your signature)

_____

(Today's date)

CHAPTER ONE: I Have an Idea! Nine Ways to Write a Book

You have a great idea for a book, but you're not sure how to proceed. Should you just sit down and start writing? You could. Many writers use this method, which is called "pantsing." This is when you just write without any real plan as we used to do in school with creative writing assignments.

The flip side is called "plotting." This is when you create an outline of your book before you begin writing. This is the most popular of the two approaches. Think of it like using a road map. Do you just set out for your destination without any idea how to get there or do you study a map first? Some folks do figure it out as they go, but most of us check a map and figure out the best route.

For all you pantsers, you can always change your mind and create an outline at any point in the process if you get stuck. Hopefully, if and when you get stuck, you'll have a good grasp of your story, how you want it to end, and your cast of characters, so plotting will help you pull it all together.

You can get stuck even if you have your plot outlined, believe me, but plotting reduces the chances of getting stuck, or at the very least, keeps you from straying so far off track that you can't find your way back. There are several ways to go about outlining your book. There are nine ways that I know of that you can go about outlining your book. This chapter is going to reveal all these options so that you can decide the best approach for you.

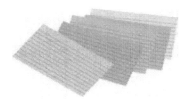

1. If you're a low-tech person like me, you may want to go with the **INDEX CARD METHOD**. Buy a bundle of index cards at the drug store or office supply store and use them to write notes for each scene and also for each character (physical traits and characteristics; see Chapter Seven for more about this). Use these scene cards

to create chapters. You should also get a large bulletin board and a box of tacks so that you can properly display your index cards and delete or add or move scenes around. I have a two-sided bulletin board, so I put all the character information on one side and the scene cards on the other side.

2. The second choice is the **SNOWFLAKE METHOD**. You start with a single sentence that describes your novel. Then you take that sentence and turn it into a paragraph that summarizes your novel. Now you insert information about your characters, such as their names, goals, conflicts, motivation, traits, and story line. The final step is to go back and make each sentence into a paragraph and fully flesh out your characters (quirks, dialect, physical traits, backstory, etc.). www.advancedfictionwriting.com/articles/snowfl ake-method

3. Another approach is the **SPREADSHEET METHOD**. Microsoft Excel works well for organizing information, such as your table of contents, cast of characters, and mapping out scenes. Microsoft Word should be used for writing. www.ehow.com/how_6679085_write-book-using-excel.html

4. There's also the **TRELLO METHOD**. Trello is a free project-managing tool that you can use to store and sort all your book scenes. You can write each idea on a virtual card. This is the same principle as #1 (index cards) only these cards are on your computer rather than a bulletin board. You move them around under different headings in order to outline the plot. This is a great alternative to index cards for those who tend to do most of their writing outside the home. Using this method means that your index cards are always with you for quick reference in case you get an idea while you're away from home. trello.com/angelabooth/5

5. The **SCRIVENER METHOD** is hugely popular, but this software requires a good deal of time to learn how to properly use it. You can play around with it and learn on your own, find free online tutorials, or by buying a tutorial program. I have included a link to a short tutorial written by Sara Whitford, who is my co-host on *A Writer's Journey: From Blank Page to Published*. She loves Scrivener and she wrote a great post about it on sarawhitford.com/favorite-writing-tips-3-how-i-use-scrivener. You can find lots of information about Scrivener by simply doing a keyword search. Be aware that this is software

you must buy so make sure you check out some tutorials before you decide. Also, make sure you have the operating system required to support this software, which is available for Macintosh and Windows.

6. **ResophNotes METHOD** is another software option similar to Scrivener, but I've heard that it has less clutter than Scrivener and is just plain easier to use. Still, some folks say that you can't beat Scrivener, so be sure to check out both and then decide which you think is best for you. One big plus with ResophNotes is that it's free. Also, I understand that it interfaces very well and takes almost no time to learn.
www.resoph.com/ResophNotes/Welcome.html

7. Another free software option is **EVERNOTE METHOD**. Similar options include Dark Room (clone of WriteRoom but made for Windows whereas WriteRoom is only for Macs, dark-

room.en.softonic.com, free), Write Monkey (free writing app that does not require installation, writemonkey.en.softonic.com), Notepad+ (notepad-plus-plus.org/download/v6.7.8.2.html, free) and Zen Writer (download.cnet.com/ZenWriter/3000-2351_4-75416129.html, free trial but you have to buy the software if you decide to use it). evernote.com

8. **THE THREE-ACT METHOD** is another way to go. Being a low-tech gal, this one really appeals to me. The idea is that you start with Act One (your idea) and decide how you want your story to end (Act Three) and then figure out how you're going to get from beginning to end (Act Two).

9. The last method I know of is the **HALF HOUR NOVEL OUTLINE METHOD.** This is when you ask yourself six questions and the answers to these six questions form the basis of your outline. I found this approach on www.creativewritingnow.com:

Who is your main character (protagonist)?

What is the goal your main character wants/needs to achieve?

What will be the major conflict standing in the way of achieving this goal?

Where and when will your story take place?

What is your genre? (mystery, fantasy, science fiction, romance, etc.)

What action will occur? (battle, race, journey, etc.)

Chapter Summary: Find the outlining method that works best for you. If you try one approach and it doesn't seem to be working, change gears. Try a different method. Sara was halfway through writing her novel when she discovered Scrivener. I have used several of these methods as I found that different methods work well for me according to what kind of book I'm writing, such as whether it's fiction or nonfiction and how much of the book I have already conceptualized by the time I sit down to write it. You don't have to pick a method and marry it. Just because you choose a certain method for your first book doesn't mean you have to go with that for your next project or even stick with it throughout the first book.

"If you can't tell yourself what your story is in one or two sentences, you're already running into trouble.
—Gerald Petievich

CHAPTER TWO: The Time Is Now! Making a Commitment to Writing

As with anything else, you have to make a serious commitment to writing if you want to be successful. But writing is a solitary endeavor, and it can be hard for new writers to get in the habit of sitting down every single day and doing it. It is doubly hard if you are writing a book in your spare time because most of us do not have spare time.

Writing in our spare time is how nearly all of us started out. I wasn't able to quit my job until my third book was published. Actually, I had two jobs: a full-time job and a part-time teaching position at the college. Plus, I was accepting freelance writing assignments to build my reputation. I thought that when I "hit it big" I could take things a bit easier. Ha! Instead of things slackening up, my responsibilities have grown significantly. I still teach part-time at the college because I love teaching. I still accept freelance writing assignments and speaking engagements because they are good for my career. To promote my work, I participate in book tours and media interviews, as well as host two podcasts, maintain two websites, write four blogs, and help with a family business. And on top of all of that, I have to research new book projects *and* market my latest book release *and* continually promote all my backlist titles. So I do know a bit about being busy and there never being enough time for all that needs to be done. But I am organized and good with time management, which is essential for writers, at least in my opinion.

If you have trouble in these areas or you're having trouble committing to a regular routine of writing, you may need more accountability. Some writers find it helpful to be part of a writing community. This can be a local writers group that meets bi-weekly or once a month. Members bring the pages they have written since the last meeting so that other members can critique their work. Those pages will be critiqued at the next meeting after members have had a chance to read them. Pages you turned in during your last meeting will be discussed during the current meeting. But even though you are always a week behind, you always must have something ready to submit. You are also expected to take the time to critique other members' writing. If you're not willing to do this, then you can't participate.

You can check with your local library to find out about local writers' groups. Often groups meet there or at a local bookstore. Meetup.com and Google ("writing group" and "your city") are good resources for finding writing groups.

If there's not a group in your area or you just don't feel it's a good fit for you, start your own group. Make sure you have like-minded members. By this, I mean folks who are seriously committed. This is not meant to be a social club (like a book club) or a hobby for bored housewives or retirees. You want members who can help you to grow as a writer. You want folks who will push you to be the best writer you can be. You can find information online to help get you started.

Some writers like the intensity of a writing residence program. This is when you live "in residence" and do nothing but write for the duration, which can be for one week, one month, or a semester.

There are some helpful online resources, such as www.WritersCafe.org, Writer's Digest University's online writing classes, www.writersonlineworkshops.com, and the Writing Challenge. You can join the challenge at any time, www.writingchallenge.org, but if you want to follow them on Twitter, be advised that their hashtags change monthly, such as #OctoberWritingChallenge or #MayWritingChallenge.

The Writing Challenge was founded by Kristy Acevedo. She is a teacher and wanted to finish her first novel over the summer, but felt she needed a support system. So she started the group, which morphed into something much bigger and more lasting than she anticipated. Members cheer each other on and hold each other accountable to write 500 words a day. This can be in the form of writing a first draft, working on revisions, or anything that furthers your writing goal, such as social media or book research.

There are other options you can find by doing a little research, such as National Novel Writing Month (NaNoWriMo). This thirty-day writing challenge takes places every November: www.nanawrimo.org. While I'm not a fan of this approach, it does have *some* merit for *some* writers.

Joining the organization for your genre can be beneficial for connecting with other writers and learning about special events, workshops, and much more. Here are some groups, but you can do an online search to find more if your genre is not included:

Historical Novel Society, Mystery Writers of America, Romance Writers of America, Science Fiction and

Fantasy Writers of America, Sisters in Crime, National Association of Memoir Writers, Erotica Readers and Writers, and Society of Children's Book Writers and Illustrators.

If you write nonfiction, you can join the local chapter (or start one) of Nonfiction Authors Association, http://nonfictionauthorsassociation.com/join/.

Tips for starting your own writing group from six successful groups:

Keep meetings fun! Laugh a lot!

Keep groups small because smaller groups have more time for critiquing. When a member leaves be sure to accept a new member as it is important not to become stagnant. Be honest and kind. Keep criticism constructive. Make the commitment to write and attend weekly meetings. Have guidelines. Be clear and consistent what you offer members and what you expect. You should have a welcome packet that includes a mission statement for new members. Write!

Chapter Summary: A good support system is crucial to being successful. Some folks need it more than others. Not only does joining a group, such as a local writers group or online group, such as this writing challenge, offer encouragement, but it also keeps you accountable. When working alone, it is important to have a goal and deadline. So come up with a plan, make a serious commitment, and stick with it. If you're new to writing, it is a good idea to attend at least one or two writer's conferences or workshops, such as Writer's Digest University, or you can find a lengthy list of options on writing.shawguides.com

The Shack **was self-published by a first-time author and became a bestseller with millions of copies sold.**

Stephen King says, *"You only need two things to be a great writer. You have to read a lot and write a lot."*

CHAPTER THREE: Two Keys to Being Successful at Writing Nonfiction

1. **Be an expert**. You can't write (or at least you shouldn't write) about something you don't know a lot about. You should be recognized as an expert in your field and have credentials to prove it to include in your book bio, media interviews, and pitch letters.

John Grisham was a southern lawyer so his first book was a legal thriller set in the South. Martha Stewart, the notorious domestic diva, writes about home decorations, cooking, and crafts. Arthur Frommer and Rick Steves are travel experts so they write about travel. John Le Carre (David Cornwell) once served in the British Foreign Office so he writes spy novels. Robin Cook is a doctor, so he writes medical thrillers. Jackie Collins (sister of famous actress, Joan Collins) writes what she knows best—Hollywood. Celebrity chefs, such as Rachel Ray and the Barefoot Contessa, write cook books. Supermodels, such as Heidi Klum and Victoria Nixon, write books about beauty. If you are an expert on a subject, such as fitness, finance, marketing, travel, coaching, or children you are qualified to write books on those subjects. If you are not considered an expert in your field then you are not qualified to write a "how-to" book.

2. **Write well**. Your work should be well presented. This means it should be edited, organized, and properly formatted. Do your research. Get your facts straight.

Bill Wasik, author of *And Then There's This: How Stories Live and Die in Viral Culture* says, "The first tip is that readers expect books to be exhaustive on their subjects. That doesn't mean they want the books to be long—it means that they expect that you will cover all the basic ground that needs to be covered to understand the subject, even if they know some of it already. This piece of advice may or may not be relevant to your subject. In my case, with a very idiosyncratic book on viral culture, it led to people asking me at readings why I hadn't included an analysis of X or Y viral phenomenon in my book. 'Because you already know about it,' the magazine guy in me always wanted to respond. But in the book world, people want to see you mention the stuff they already know, at least in passing (or to knock it down). Otherwise, how can it claim to be a *book* on the subject? It's worth taking that point of view seriously."

Always verify your information is correct and up-to-date by using multiple resources, such as interviewing experts, contacting the historical society, and using databases, such as:

Grolier Online (features encyclopedias and newspapers)
HeritageQuest (genealogy, local histories, etc.)
OnFile (periodical and journals)
CultureGrams (reports on 200 countries)
ProQuest (e.g. will tell you what the weather was in Manhattan on June 1, 1953)
CDC
Census Bureau
Questia
Google Books
Docusearch

For a complete list of online databases check out
https://en.wikipedia.org/wiki/List_of_online_databases

Nonfiction Authors Association is a great resource for those writing biographies, memoirs, how-to books, travel books, and manuals or textbooks. Members may attend workshops and webinars, as well as benefit from lots of other resources. It is free to join, www.nonfictionauthorsassociation.com. They have local chapters in many cities with regular meetings.

Chapter Summary: Write what you know and know what you write. Research well. Write well.

Peter Connors, author of *Growing Up Dead*, nails it. *"Nonfiction shouldn't mean poorly written. Writing is writing and art always counts. Make your book beautiful to read and you're more likely to communicate your messages to your reader."*

CHAPTER FOUR: Essential Elements of a Novel

Regardless of what method you use to outline your book or what genre you are writing, there must be three parts (also referred to as the Three Acts) to your book:

> **Part I: Beginning.** *Once Upon a Time…* This is when you set up your story. In other words, you are revealing the conflict. You must "hook" your reader right away. During Part I, which is the first 25 percent of the book, it is your job to tell the reader what your story is about and introduce your protagonist.
>
> **Part II: Middle of story.** Your story (crisis/complications) unfolds during this part or act of your book. Pacing is critical since this is the main part of your story and covers about 50 percent of your book.
>
> **Part III: End of story.** During the last 25 percent of your book, you are reaching your story's conclusion. This needs to be a strong finish with a big climax that satisfies the reader.

Here are a couple of examples of the Three-Act Structure:

Cinderella

Act I: Cinderella's wicked stepmother won't let her go to the ball.

Act II: Fairy Godmother helps Cinderella go to the ball where she meets Prince Charming, falls in love, and loses her glass slipper.

Act III: Cinderella returns to her life of drudgery waiting on her stepmother and sisters. Prince Charming finds her and takes her away from her life of servitude. They live happily ever after.

Star Wars

Part I: Princess Leia is captured. Luke Skywalker's family is murdered, so he joins Obi-Wan to save the princess and destroy the Death Star.

Part II: Luke becomes a Jedi knight and joins forces with Han Solo and Chewbacca.

Part III: Good battles evil and good prevails. The Force destroys the Death Star. Princess Leia is saved and all is right with the world once again.

First, let's look at the beginning. How do you "hook" the reader? You've got to grab their attention ASAP!

Here are the three most common techniques:

1. <u>Pique the reader's curiosity</u>. Why is something happening? How did it happen? What is going on? Draw readers in by making them wonder about something. Why is the protagonist afraid of her husband? How did the protagonist end up in a particular situation? How is the protagonist going to get out of a bad situation?

2. <u>Introduce a conflict or problem</u>. The great thing about introducing conflict is that there is no limit. It can be big or small and frequent or infrequent—but you must have it. You can introduce it right away or build towards it.

3. <u>Begin with a bang!</u> Start with action and then catch the readers up on what they need to know as the story progresses.

Setting. Besides hooking your reader, you need to establish the setting of your story. Where and when does your story take place? The South Carolina Lowcountry in summer in the present day? Fifteenth-century Taiwan? Los Angeles in the 1970s? Colorado in the winter during the Gold Rush?

Give this some serious thought as the setting is critical to any story. There should be a reason your story is taking place in an abandoned lighthouse on the Georgia coast or on a spaceship traveling the galaxy in 2050 or in the remote woods of Maine. Make sure your reader can easily discern where your story is set and why. Setting descriptions are critical to connecting the reader to your story.

Your main character. Your protagonist *must* be introduced at the beginning of your story (Act I). In addition to revealing your protagonist and setting, your reader should be able to grasp what kind of story this is by your book description/summary and the first few pages. Whatever genre you are writing, from erotica to horror, your reader should be able to recognize the genre fairly quickly.

Part II (middle) is where most writers run into trouble. It usually happens around page 50–70. They hit the wall. This is referred to as the middle lull. Hopefully, this will not happen to you, but if it does, refer to Chapters Four and Ten, which deal with this issue. Just remember that by the middle of your book, the plot should be thickening and subplots should be introduced. The reader should be discovering the protagonist's backstory and the stakes should be getting higher. The characters should be dealing with major challenges and obstacles. The reader should be heavily invested in your story by this point.

See Chapter Eleven to learn more about **Part III** or the conclusion of your story.

Chapter Summary: Write the story you want to read. Before you start writing, you should know your beginning, middle, and end (three acts). Hook your readers right away. Let them know what the story is about, who your protagonist is, and where your story is set as soon as possible.

"An author knows his landscape best; he can stand around, smell the wind, get a feel for his place."
—Tony Hillerman

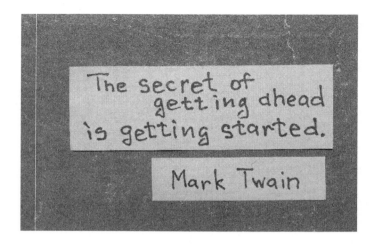

CHAPTER FIVE: Can You Answer These Four Questions?

Okay, so no matter where you are in the process, whether you've finished your first draft or just a few chapters, it's time to evaluate. In other words, it's time to ask the tough questions starting with, "Have you written a story worth sharing?"

What do I mean by this? The goal of every writer should be to write a breakout novel. This means it will be successful, not just published. This is an important distinction!

You need four elements to achieve a breakout novel:

1. Plausibility.

Is this plot realistic but not obvious?

The plot needs to be clear to the reader, but the ending shouldn't be apparent.

2. **Conflict.**

   What is the conflict?

   There *must* be conflict. You should complicate your plot if your conflict is overly predictable, too easily solved, or lacks sufficient tension. Formula: Conflict x Tension = Good Story!

3. **Originality.**

   What makes your story unique?

   These days everything has pretty much been done in books, movies, and television. So it is a challenge to come up with an original story line, but the good news is that it doesn't have to be completely original. In fact, it can be the same old story *but* with an original approach.

   Note: You'll have to address this twist in your pitch letter to an agent and editor. Plus, it needs to be the focal point of your synopsis. Remember that you need to be able to summarize your story in one or two sentences.

4. **Gut Emotional Appeal.**

   What kind of response are you expecting from readers?

   Your story must provoke some kind of emotional reaction from the reader. It can be sadness, anger, curiosity, sympathy, outrage, fear, empathy, or mixed emotions, but it must elicit a response. In other words, the reader must be invested in your story and its characters.

Sit down with whatever you've written and honestly answer each of these questions:

> *Q. Is this plot realistic but not obvious?*
> A.
> *Q. What is the conflict?*
> A.
> *Q. What makes your story unique?*
> A.
> *Q. What kind of response are you expecting from readers?*
> A.

These are good questions to pose to your beta readers (early reviewers) when you get to that stage. You need to make sure that the reader can answer these questions with the responses you're anticipating. If your beta reader cannot tell you what the conflict is, it's revision time. Run, don't walk to your computer! Study popular books in the same genre with these four questions in mind. Learn how these authors achieved these critical elements.

Author Steve Berry (*The Amber Room*) had eighty-seven rejections for five different manuscripts before his agent found a publisher.

Some more things to consider:

What twists could I add to the plot?

What consequences could arise from this conflict?

How can I make my story's setting reflect the conflict?

Have I done a good job with my characters?

Does the reader understand their motives and actions?

Have I fully revealed their physical and behavioral traits and quirks or disorders?

Have I done enough research to tell my story correctly?

Can I add anything to make my story better?

Be sure to avoid clichés when it comes to character names, setting, character traits, and language.

Chapter Summary: Make sure your story is worth telling. It takes four things to create a breakout novel: plausibility, conflict, originality, and emotional response. There are lots of great writing resources, but my favorites (besides this reference, of course!) are *Am Writing* by Stephen King, *How I Write* by Janet Evanovich, and *How to Write a Breakout Novel* by Donald Maass.

Newsweek Editor, Nancy Cooper, says it best *"You just start working and you keep working 'til it's done. That's all there is to it; no mystery."*

CHAPTER SIX: It's All About the View

No, I'm not talking about the daytime talk show. I'm talking about *point of view*. Before you start writing, you have to decide how you're going to tell your story. Or rather who is going to tell your story?

The two main ways are as **first person** (I) and **third person** (he/she). Yes, there is a second person POV, but it is rarely used because it is a difficult concept to successfully achieve.

In the first-person narrative, the protagonist tells the story. The protagonist is your main character. This is also the easiest way to do it as you are writing as if the events are happening to you. For the same reason, it is easier for the reader to follow. Be aware that the only way the reader can know how any other characters are feeling or what's happening to them is if this information has been revealed to the protagonist.

In the third person, both the writer and reader know what is going on with all or most of the characters in the story. A third-person narrative can stick with a single character at center stage (restricted/limited third person) or there can be multiple points of view (omniscient).

FYI: WHEN YOU CHANGE POV, YOU MUST CHANGE SCENES OR CHAPTERS.

So how do you decide which POV is best? Here are some guidelines:

First person is best for a small cast of characters, a simple story, one where you want to use quirky language and tell it from one character's perspective or if you want your readers to connect with one character. This character telling the story is typically your protagonist. This is a popular POV but the downside is that the reader only sees and knows what the main character sees and knows.

Third person (omniscient) is best for revealing what's going on with a lot of characters so if you have a large cast of characters, this would be the way to go. If you want to insert any information that would be outside your character's thoughts or if you don't want to establish too close a connection between the main character and the reader, this is the best POV. It is said that the narrator is "God-like" since the third person omniscient point of view is all-knowing.

Third person (restricted) allows the action to be seen through a few characters rather than just one as is the case with first person point of view. This gives the author greater flexibility than first person but keeps it simpler than omniscient third person. With restricted third-person point of view both the writer and reader know what is going on in the heads of many different characters.

To learn more about first person POV, study best-selling book series, *Hunger Games* (Suzanne Collins) and *Twilight* (Stephanie Meyer).

To learn more about third person (omniscient) read the classic *Lord of the Rings* (J.K. Tolkien) and hugely popular *A Series of Unfortunate Events* (Lemony Snicket).

To get a better grasp on third person (limited or restricted), have you heard of *Harry Potter* (J. K. Rowling) and *Song of Ice and Fire* (George R.R. Martin)?

A novel that successfully blends first, second, and third person point of views is *Night Circus* (Erin Morgenstern).

Most genres use multiple POV with the exception of mystery/suspense/thriller/crime/creative nonfiction, which typically stick with first person.

FYI: It is not uncommon for writers to change POV after they have finished a first draft.

Chapter Summary: Decide your POV. Stick with one POV during a scene. If you need to change POV, you need to end the scene or chapter and start a new scene or chapter to let the reader know there's been a change.

It took nine years and fourteen drafts before Harley Jane Kozak's *Dating Dead Men* was ready to be pitched so don't give up. Her fourth book was released this year.

Mark Frauenfelder, author of *The Mad Professor,* says it best, *"Don't forget to write the book that you want to read."*

CHAPTER SEVEN: Who's Your Protagonist?

Most stories are character-driven because your characters are what brings your story to life, and how your characters do this is through action and dialogue. You need a lot of action and dialogue in a novel—show and tell. You may have heard the mantra "Show, don't tell!" but I believe a good book does both. While there is great debate over which is more important—the characters, story, or dialogue—it is best to carefully consider all three as you write.

A good rule of thumb is that all prominent characters and settings need to be introduced within the first 25 percent of your book. Also, your major plot should rock the world of your main character (protagonist) and force a reaction from him or her within the first 25 percent of your book.

The most important thing is that the reader needs to feel something towards your protagonist whether it's disgust or empathy or love or hate. You must evoke some sort of response. If readers are cold or lukewarm towards your main character, it is going to be hard for them to care about what happens to the protagonist and subsequently about your story.

Also, your protagonist needs to grow and change either for the better or worse but there must be substantial change by the end of the book. Furthermore, your protagonist needs to be quirky, out of the ordinary (larger-than-life), imperfect (flawed), and complex.

Here are some questions you need to answer as you create your protagonist:

Is it he or she?

How old is he or she?

What will he/she lose or gain during the story? What will he/she sacrifice? How will this affect him/her?

What does the character want? What motivates him/her?

What are his/her bad habits or vices or flaws? Good habits or strengths? How do these flaws and strengths affect the story?

Is he good-looking? Is she pretty? Hair color? Hair style? Weight? Build? Complexion?

Is he arrogant? Is she snobbish?

Is he/she funny or serious?

Who is he/she close to? Does he/she have a BFF and will the BFF play a prominent role in the novel or is he/she a loner or will true love or friendship be discovered during the course of the story?

What kind of disposition does he/she have? Is he/she a journey or destination kind of person?

Does he/she have any pets?

Where does he/she live? What does that say about him/her?

What are his/her hobbies?

What are his/her passions?

Does he/she have a job?

Is lack of money or too much money a problem for him/her?

What are his/her achievements?

Does he/she have children? Are his/her feelings towards the child or children clear? Is he/she a good parent?

Is he/she married or divorced or in a committed relationship or single?

What about his/her sex life?

What's his/her background (backstory)? Where does he/she come from? What is his/her family dynamic? Estranged? Close? Deceased?

Is he/she keeping any secrets? What are we allowed to know about them?

Does he/she have ambitions or dreams we need to know about? A dark past we should know about? Maybe he/she can't form close relationships because of something that happened to him/her in the past?

How does he/she speak? With a southern drawl or has an accent or talks too fast? Mannerisms?

Does he/she have special features or striking attributes, such as bluest eyes you've ever seen or freckles or a scar on the right cheek?

Is he/she a terrible cook or OCD about a clean house or forgetful?

How does he/she dress?

Is he/she compassionate or aloof?

Where does he/she live? City? Small town? Farm? Lighthouse? Ranch? Trailer park?

What kind of car does he/she drive?

What is the character's greatest fear? What is the character trying to hide?

One technique employed by some writers is to interview their protagonist. What does this mock interview reveal? The important thing is that you have a clear understanding of your protagonist and are able to convey this to your readers. Your composite of characters should be diversified with each possessing a different persona and with different kinds of relationships and interactions. How you share this information depends on the POV you choose.

If you have an antagonist (and this is generally a good idea), you need to do the same process as you have done for your protagonist for him/her. This should also be done for all of your characters unless they are one-dimensional.

Stanford University released a study recently that proves that walking boosts creativity by 60 percent and that doing it outdoors is best for sparking your imagination—so if you're struggling with your writing go take a walk!

You may add questions to this sheet or delete anything you don't feel is relevant. It is up to you and your genre and your story line as to how much you want to share about your character.

Character Interview

Name:

Hometown:

Location of story:

Type of residence (where a person lives reveals something about his/her character and/or circumstances, such as an apartment, mansion, cottage, halfway house, lighthouse, homeless, multiple homes, or trailer):

Parents:

Siblings:

Children and/or grandchildren:

Ethnicity and skin color:

Education/skills:

Job:

Status (single/widowed/divorced/married/engaged):

Friends:

Enemies:

Personality (positive or negative outlook):

Conflict (what is his/her problem):

Secret or secrets (is he hiding something or in denial about someone):

Backstory (abused/scarred emotionally/mental issues):

Physical traits (height/eye color/hair style/hair color/attractive/plain):

Distinguishing marks (birthmarks, scars, tattoos, piercings):

Fears:

Failures:

Achievements:

Hobbies:

Vehicle:

Pet(s):

Quirks:

Chapter Summary: You need to put a lot of thought into your character. He/she has a huge burden to bear in the success of your novel. Make sure you have done a good job of making sure your protagonist comes across the way you want him/her to, such as being a sympathetic character or understanding his motive.

"Rather than describing my characters, I try to come up with actions to show what they're like."
—Jude Deveraux

CHAPTER EIGHT: Dealing with Distractions

We all have things that pull us away from writing, especially when we work at home. That's life. I think that Amy Sue Nathan put it best when she wrote, *"Writing is done in the time we make, not the time we find."* (*Writer's Digest*, July/Aug '15).

Here are five ways to make the most of your time:

1. Discover your best creative time. For some writers this is 6:00 a.m. and for others it's 11:00 p.m. I write best late at night. When I sit down to write, I write for a minimum of two to four hours as that works best for me. I have found that late at night I suffer the least interruptions, so that is the main reason I choose to write at that time. Also, I'm not a morning person. I'm a night owl so I will be more creative at night than in the

morning. What's your best time? When are you most energetic and creative?

2. Discover your best creative space. This may be a nook you've created in your garage or basement or laundry room or in a corner of the attic. If you can, turn your storage shed or gardening shed into a writer's workshop. Maybe writing on your deck or porch or patio works well for you. Or do you have a designated office or study area? Can you hang a "do not disturb" sign on your bedroom door and use that space? Can you go somewhere else if it's not possible to work at home, such as the library or a café or the park?

3. The important thing is not the size of the space, but that you create a designated space where you can regularly write. This must be your time and your space. No interlopers allowed. No kids. No pets. No spouse. No television. No music. No phone. No emails. No social media. No eating. No distractions. The point is to stay focused *intensely* on the writing. I have a fan in my office that creates a soothing sound (white noise) and drowns out all other noises that may distract me.

4. Get your family on board. Your family will probably stick to your rules if you just ask. Before we start each recording for *A Writer's Journey: From Blank Page to Published*, Sara tells her son that she is about to do our show and that he needs to remember to keep quiet until she tells him otherwise. Then she gives him a chance to ask any questions or get whatever he needs to

settle down. Even though he is only eleven years old, he understands and obeys once asked. Don't just get your physical space ready, get your mind ready. Get psyched. Get ready to be creative. You must get started and develop a routine and stick with it. Author Jessica Keener says, *"I guess it's like exercising. The more you do it, the more it just becomes something you do."*

5. Bribe yourself if need be. I'm sure you've bribed your children on occasion. "You can have ice cream if you eat all your vegetables." "You can watch television if you finish your homework." Employ a reward system that works for you. If you achieve your daily goal, reward yourself with a special treat, such as a glass of wine, a chocolate bar, a concert, or a trip to the park with your pooch, playtime with your kids, workout at the gym, or take a nap or a long bubble bath, meet friends for dinner or curl up with a good book for an hour or two.

TIP: Be sure to set a writing goal. Come up with a word count or page count, such as 500 words a day or three pages. Hopefully, your most creative time will also be when your schedule permits it, but you may have to make adjustments because of the confines of your schedule, such as writing when your kids are at school or at night when you get home from work.

A U T H O R
A T
W O R K **Two Things You Need to Know to Become a Better Writer...**

There are two ways to become a better writer: write a lot and read a lot. Reading makes you a better writer on so many levels. It shows you what works and how and why. It takes place on a subconscious level for the most part (except for those "aha" moments), but it's happening nonetheless. This comes out in your writing. And the more you write, the better you'll get at it. Remember that practice makes perfect.

Be sure to set yourself up for the next day. When I finish a writing session, I make sure I leave something to write, such as the final paragraph or the rest of the chapter. I know what I want to happen, but I walk away because I know I will be obsessed with finishing that chapter or introducing a new character or writing the rest of a fight scene. Otherwise, I may invent a distraction. I have been known to do everything from grooming the dog to reorganizing the pantry just to avoid writing, especially if I don't know what I want to do next. So, the trick is to leave yourself something to write—something you will feel compelled to finish.

It comes down to making writing a part of your daily routine. That way it will be weird *not* to do it. I have forced myself to write so many times that I am now in the habit of writing on a daily basis. I have writer's remorse if a day starts to slip away, and I haven't written anything that day.

Time management is also crucial. Many of us are guilty of taking a quick break to check emails or posting a picture on our favorite social media but then that morphs into two hours tweeting and posting.

You need to make up your mind that when you sit down to write, that's what you'll do. No cheating. Set a timer so that you're not "allowed" to do anything for at least one hour but write. If you can't go one hour a day without social media, consider professional help.

Seriously, if you need help overcoming social media distractions, there are resources that can be helpful. **Anti-social.cc** (an app that blocks social media for a pre-designated time) or **selfcontrolapp.com** or **chrome.google.com/webstore** (to find stay focused tools) as well as www.coffitivity.com and www.rainymood.com.

For those who need extra help (and you know who you are) check out www.writeordie.com. I love this idea. If you don't achieve your goal, reminders appear: gentle (reminder box pops up), normal (irritating sounds until you start typing again), or kamikaze (what you already wrote disappears until you start typing again).

A good way to handle social media is by using tools that manage it, such as Hootsuite, Everypost, Buffer, and SocialOomph. Set up an account with one of these sites and devote an hour or two a week creating and timing tweets and then forget about it. This is how I deal with Facebook and Twitter, and I love it. Granted, some interaction is necessary since it is social media, but it keeps social media from being a huge time suck.

Chapter Summary: If you figure out your best time of day and best space to write and then set a daily goal, then you are less likely to get distracted either by accident or intentionally.

"A goal is a dream with a deadline."
— Napoleon Hill

CHAPTER NINE: Three Keys to Writing a Breakout Novel

In my opinion, this is the most important chapter in this book. If you don't get this right, it's like trying to bake a cake without flour. You can bake a cake without flour, but it isn't going to taste good. You can write a story without mastering this stuff, but it isn't going to be a story worth reading.

But don't worry. I have made this easy for you. I have come up with a formula based on all the things I've learned over the years in writing classes, blogs, conferences, workshops, writing references, and webinars. Just remember the three Ps:

PLOT

PACING

PROTAGONIST

In Chapter Seven, I discuss everything you need to know about your protagonist and proper character development so be sure to study that chapter. That leaves plot and pacing. Let's start with the plot.

All you need to remember is: *plot = goal*. What is the *goal* of your protagonist? In other words, what is your protagonist trying to achieve? Sure, you can have subplots, but what is your main plot? For example, best-selling author Janet Evanovich's Stephanie Plum series features Stephanie Plum as a bond enforcement agent. So her goal (or main plot) is always to catch the skip or FTA (failure to appear) so she can pay her rent and buy another car since her car always gets destroyed at some point in the story.

Your plot should include the three Cs. Be sure to refer to Chapter Four for more about the Three Acts or Three Parts of a novel:

CONFLICT (Act One)

COMPLICATIONS (Act Two)

CLIMAX/CONCLUSION (Act Three)

Using this same example, Stephanie Plum has all kinds of other stuff going on while she is trying to track down the FTA, such as family drama and relationship issues.

Her family doesn't understand why she has chosen to be a bounty hunter when she could have been a respectable suburban housewife and mother, so she is often at odds with her mother over her lifestyle. She is torn between two men throughout this series: her sometimes boyfriend and hunky cop, Joe Morelli, and a tall, dark, and mysterious man named Ranger, who owns a private security company. She sometimes works for him when she needs rent money. As you can see, the author has created lots of conflict and complications that always culminate in a thrilling conclusion.

Just remember, the plot should thicken. In other words, tension must build. This brings us to pacing. On average, a novel is 70,000–120,000 words, depending on the genre. For example, historical fiction tends to be longer in length than romance, young adult, or chick lit. Keep in mind that whatever method you use to write your book (such as index cards or Scrivener) be sure to pace accordingly. So for simplicity's sake, let's say there will be a total of 100 scenes. This means that 25 of those should be in the first 25 percent of the book, 50 scenes should be in the middle 50 percent of the book, and 25 scenes should be in the last 25 percent of the book.

Not all scenes have the same purpose in your story. Some will be a much bigger deal than other ones whose purpose may only be to reveal a small piece of information to the readers, such as a character trait or setting up a bigger scene. This means that length of the scene and subsequent pacing will be different, according to the significance of a specific scene.

If you're still uncertain about pacing, here's what you need to know in a nutshell.

Pacing = Tension

Pacing can make or break a story. It's all about controlling the speed at which a story is told. Pacing is how you control the flow of information given to the reader and often depends on the genre. For example, in a cozy mystery there better be a murder within the first few pages. In historical fiction, the pacing can be more leisurely. No matter what kind of book you're writing, you don't want to go so fast as to leave readers confused or disoriented. On the flip side, you don't want to go so slow as to lose the interest of your reader. If you remember the aforementioned 25/50/25 formula, you will be good to go.

What about the Prologue?

Should an author add one to his story if he doesn't have one? Prologues are among the most misunderstood and abused writing techniques.

A prologue should only be used if you need to explain key information that doesn't fit into the same timeline or time flow as the rest of your book. Otherwise, it is best to begin with Chapter One.

If you're in doubt, leave it out.

Additionally, there are three techniques you can use to help with your plot, protagonist, and pacing:

Foreshadowing is a literary device used by writers to hint about what's to come later in the story. The purpose of foreshadowing is to build anticipation and add dramatic tension to a story. If done correctly, foreshadowing is the best tool in a writer's toolbox. Not only does foreshadowing add so much to the story, but it can make extraordinary events acceptable to readers as they have been mentally prepped for them. In other words, something that may have seemed questionable or preposterous to readers has validity because you have told them it was coming. Foreshadowing can be achieved in many ways, such as prophecies, omens, symbolism, and red herrings—when the writer provides false clues or deliberately misleads the reader. This creates a wonderful surprise and a more suspenseful climax for the reader.

The backstory is used to reveal important information relevant to the story and characters. It is a good way to introduce necessary information, but it is important to remember that by inserting a backstory you are stopping the momentum of your story. You are actually moving backward, hence the term "backstory." This means this technique should be used effectively and sparingly. A backstory can be introduced through flashbacks, dialogue, or character musings or recollections, but your story should never start off with a backstory. It should be information that is cleverly weaved into the story well after it is underway. The mistake of rookie writers is thinking that the reader needs to know all kinds of information immediately. Not so. In fact, it usually adds to the story to dribble this information out as you go along so as to keep the reader on his toes and invested in your story. If writing a series, a backstory is very important. Each novel should stand alone in terms of plot but needs to have the same backstory. For example, in the Harry Potter series, Harry's past is the key to the story. He has to find out who murdered his parents and what he's going to do about it. The backstory should be set up in book one of your series but revisited in all the books in the series so that new readers can learn what they need to know. Many rookie writers make the mistake of thinking that flashbacks and backstory are one and the same. Not so. Flashbacks can hint at backstories, but they are not backstories. The character has a flashback that reveals information (backstory) the reader needs to know. They are quick, hence the name "flashback." Something that is currently happening should be the catalyst or trigger for the flashback, such as running into someone from the character's past who reminds him/her of someone or some event he/she hadn't thought of in years or witnessing something that reminds him/her of similar events from his/her past, such as a murder or an accident.

Dialogue should always move your story forward. Cut all dialogue that does not accomplish this goal. Another common mistake for newbie writers is writing too much extraneous dialogue. Also, be careful not to make it a monologue or what is also referred to as lengthy, static prose. This means you should avoid long-winded statements or explanations from a character. Five rules to remember about writing dialogue:

1. Dialogue should always be in quotation marks, and every new line of dialogue is indented. A new paragraph should be started every time a new person is speaking. Be careful with dialogue tags. You don't need to add "he replied" or "she said" for every line but insert a qualifier every once in a while. Don't use lots of different types of tags. It is acceptable to use "he replied" or "she said" and the occasional "she screamed" or "he whispered" so that we get the idea she is angry or that he is trying to be quiet. However, words such as exclaimed, shouted, yelled, cried, roared, shrieked, and hollered should be kept to a minimum.

2. Dialogue should reveal character information to the reader, such as a southern accent, anger, or motive. It should sound natural and authentic.

3. The conversation should be realistic, meaning it should be like real life. How often do you talk to someone without doing anything else at the same time? Almost never. So there should be activity, such as washing the dishes, smoking a cigarette, eating a meal, driving somewhere, pacing the floor, getting ready to go somewhere, preparing a meal, getting dressed, and so on.

4. Don't overuse dialogue. Remember the golden rule: *Show, don't tell.* Typically, your writing should have more action than dialogue.

5. Be careful using dialogue to reveal a backstory.

So how do you get good at writing dialogue? The best way is practice, of course. Also, read books written by best-selling authors in the same genre. Study their dialogue and see how they're doing it. Also, read your dialog out loud. Seriously! The best way to critique dialogue is to hear it. Read it to yourself or to a friend or family member. How does it sound? Does it sound authentic? Does it deliver the necessary information to the reader or does it deliver too much information? Remember that dialogue is there to move the story forward. Period.

The narration is what you are writing in between dialogue. The setting, conflict, and theme are revealed through narration and/or dialogue. You are sharing the time and place, characters and conflict through your narrative. Narration can provide as much insight into a character or scene as dialogue. Neither narration nor dialogue should be used to dump information onto the reader. A good writer carefully dribbles out information so as to satisfy a reader without telling too much at one time. You do not want to overwhelm the reader or give too much away in one scene. You want to tease and please the reader right up to the end. This is why pacing is so important.

Chapter Summary: There are three keys to novel writing: plot, pacing, and protagonist. Within your plot, there should be three Cs: conflict, complications, and climax. Use dialogue, foreshadowing, and backstory to control pacing, reveal information about the characters, and thicken the plot. If using a prologue, be sure it is necessary.

"Your novel better not be a story you're lukewarm about. You really have to think this is great."
—F. Paul Wilson

CHAPTER TEN: How to Handle Writer's Block

There are times when you're going to get stuck. Some call this "writer's block." Some say they are "creatively challenged." Others, myself included, like to say that we've "hit the wall." Whatever you choose to call it, you're in a bad place. You'll struggle as you try to carry on with your story. This is when you are at a loss how to move forward. You know how you want your story to end, but you just can't see how to get there. This is when you begin to question your plot and/or subplots, dialogue, and characters. Before you start questioning every word you wrote, stop! Before you punch the delete button, take a beat because help is here. It should bring you some small comfort to know that this happens to *all* writers. In fact, it happens quite a lot. I can think of eight ways you can "hit the wall" and what you can do about it.

1. **You have an outline, but you can't get through this one part of it.**

Actually, there are two different reasons you could be getting stuck. (1) <u>Your outline has a major flaw and you just won't admit it or haven't realized it yet</u>. What you're trying to accomplish makes no sense. If this is the case, you already know it, and it's just a matter of reworking your outline. (2) <u>Your outline is basically fine, but there's a part that you can't get past because it's not getting the job done, maybe because you can't see how to get from one scene to the next</u>. There's nothing wrong with taking a slight detour and seeing what happens. Maybe you'll find a smoother transition between those two scenes, maybe you'll figure out where your story really needs to go next. Most likely, there's something that needs to happen with your characters at this point, and you just have to keep writing and trying to hit on what that is.

2. **You're stuck in the middle and have no idea what happens next.**

You were on a roll, and you wrote a whole lot of good stuff, but when you came back to your story you find that you have no idea where this story line is going. You thought you left things in a great place to pick up the ball and keep running, and now you can't imagine what you were thinking. If it's true that you were on a roll, and now you're stuck, then chances are you just need to take a step back and give yourself a couple days to recharge. Or you may need to rethink what you already wrote. If you've tried this and you're still stuck, you need to do something to get the story moving again. Introduce a new complication (plot twist) or character. Mark Twain spent months stuck in the middle of *Huckleberry Finn* before he came up with the notion of having Huck and Jim take the wrong turn on the river and get lost.

3. **You have a terrible feeling your story took a wrong turn a while back, and you don't know how to get it back on track.**

   This is the worst. If you're absolutely sure that you've gone the wrong way, then there's no point in going forward any further. You need to go back to where you feel you derailed and start again. Yes, that means deleting all the text from that point forward. There is no easy fix in this situation.

4. **You're bored or disappointed or unsure about your main character or another key character.**

Characters that don't do anything aren't interesting characters. If this is your situation, you haven't found the thing that your characters really want, or the conflict that will spur them into action. You have some characters, but not a story, at least not yet. Keep writing and see what develops. Hopefully, you can turn it around and then go back and change dialogue or actions of a character(s) to address this issue. Once you have the new character trait or conflict, you may have an "aha!" where you know exactly how to fix the earlier text.

5. You start questioning everything about your story and don't know what to do.

Chances are the ideas aren't nearly as bad as your inner critic is telling you. But in any case, you can always fix it in rewrites. Just keep going and see where your story goes.

6. You can't think of the right words for what you're trying to convey in this one paragraph.

There's nothing wrong with spending a big block of time getting one sentence or paragraph or page right. You may feel like you're wasting time, but it's important that you get it right. It may make a difference as far as what comes next.

7. You had this cool idea in your head for this scene or story, but now that you're writing it, it's not coming out the way you thought it would or should.

Don't give up too fast. It's possible that part of your idea is a good one, but you need to rethink the execution of it. Sometimes it's helpful to try writing your story (or part of your narrative) from a different character's point of view. You may not have the right POV or maybe you haven't properly developed your protagonist.

8. You're revising your work and you can't see your way past all those blocks of text you already wrote.

Revisions are a nightmare! No doubt. You probably don't have writer's block; you're just overwhelmed trying to figure out how to fix certain glaring errors in your novel. The only way to eat an elephant is one bite at a time, so start with the first scene that needs addressing and get on with it—then do another scene and another. If you're just completely baffled how to get started, try rewriting a scene completely. You should just forget the original text and start over and then go from there.

Resources: Here are some resources to help writers who have hit the wall:

www.writersstore.com/the-writers-block-jason-rekulak

www.writersblocks.com

www.creativity-portal.com/prompts/imagination.prompt.html

Chapter Summary: Every writer hits the wall at some point. This is part of the process and nothing to be overly concerned about unless you can't get "unstuck." To nip this in the bud sooner rather than later, go through my checklist. Once you identify your problem, you can follow the solution offered for getting "unstuck." Sometimes identifying and correcting the problem is as simple as getting a fresh perspective. If you truly can't figure out what to do to move forward, walk away for a while. Remember that plot twists are a writer's friend so the solution may be to go rogue and add a doozy of a twist to your story line.

Dorothy O'Neill has written eleven books since turning seventy-nine years old.

"Writing is a fairly lonely business unless you invite people in to watch you do it, which is often distracting and then you have to ask them to leave."
—Marc Lawrence

CHAPTER ELEVEN: I'm Finished Writing My Novel! Or Am I?

In this chapter, I'm going to address the end of your book. The last part of your book is the ending or "the closer." So before you start telling everyone that you're done with your novel, be sure that's true. Here are five questions to ask yourself:

1. Is your closer a doozy? It needs to blow readers away. It should be shocking, unexpected, and exciting. Also, it should be more dramatic with a bigger climax than anything else you've written up to this point. You shouldn't have a scene earlier in your story that outshines this one.

2. Does your protagonist face his antagonist? Is there a showdown? Is the crime solved? Or does your protagonist save the day? Don't forget that

conflict makes the story and must be resolved by the end—and to the reader's satisfaction.

3. Does the closer show or tell? The resolution needs to be self-evident. You shouldn't have to rely on lengthy dialogue or a long description or character musing to get the job done. As opposed to some experts, I believe in show *and* tell, but I believe there is a time and place for both. At the end or "the closer," it is all about showing. Action speaks louder than words.

4. Are you using a backstory or flashbacks in the closer? I hope your answer is no. This part of the book needs to be about action and resolution. It is not the time and place to introduce new material. By this point, you should have set up your story so that this is not necessary. And don't change your tone or attitude or resort to gimmicks, which will most likely alienate your readers.

5. Is the conclusion logical? As discussed earlier, when talking about the story line, your conclusion must also be believable to the reader. Will your ending be acceptable for fans of this genre? For example, in a romance novel the ending must be that the boy gets the girl. In other genres, relationships don't always work out but in the traditional romance genre readers will not accept any other outcome.

More Dos and Don'ts in the Closer:

1. **Don't introduce new subplots or characters.** Anything in the last fifty pages should have been foreshadowed.
2. **Don't let it drag on and on.** Get to it. Build up your finale and then let your readers off the hook before they lose interest. Remember the role of pacing in your story.
3. **Tie up all loose ends.** Answer all questions. The only exception is if your book will be part of a series. In that case, you can leave some questions unanswered or a loose end or two so that readers will be anxious to read the next installment. Be careful though. You want to leave the door open but not leave readers hanging. You don't want them to feel betrayed or cheated like you strung them along. You simply want to leave them wanting more—eager to buy your next book.
4. **Do engage your reader.** Don't think that by the end you've done all the heavy lifting and now you can coast through the end. You need to keep readers emotionally invested until the last sentence. Give them a moment where they think "Wow!" or "Whoa! I didn't see that coming!" I love O. Henry endings. I hate

figuring out how a book's going to end by the midway point. Try to surprise and delight your readers.

5. **Have you ever read a book you just couldn't put down?** You stayed up until the middle of the night hanging onto every word. Did you feel a sense of loss when you finished it? I have read books that were so good that I was actually sad when I finished them. That's how you want *your* readers to feel. When you have folks that feel this way, you have fans for life. Readers are quite loyal. If we really like a book, we will buy more books by that author.

If you feel confident you have properly addressed all these things, then I have just one thing to say…

"CONGRATULATIONS!"

You have written a book! At least, you have written a first draft of a book. You are a writer!

Chapter Summary: So many books start with a powerful opening and then go into a moderate middle, and then peter out with a weak conclusion. Go back and review the last fifty pages of your manuscript. Be critical and ask yourself the five questions and look for the four common pitfalls. If there is a problem, it may be as simple as cutting some dialogue or inserting an action scene. Or it may require much more, but you can't be a lazy writer. You have worked too hard on your book to get sloppy at this point. Walk away for a while if you need to recharge and then tackle this final stage.

Dorothy Parker said, *"I hate writing. I love having written."*

MANUSCRIPT CHECKLIST

_____Did you read your manuscript as if you were seeing it for the *first* time?

_____Is your "opener" strong?

_____Is your "closer" strong?

_____Is your plot obvious?

_____Does every word you've written move your story forward? If not, be brutal and CUT, CUT, CUT!

_____Did you do your research? Did you get your facts straight?

_____Are your characters strong (properly developed)?

_____Is your plot strong? What about subplots?

_____Has your plot/story line been properly executed? Did you do a good job telling it?

_____Do your characters ring true? Sound authentic?

_____Do you have any transitions you need to fix?

_____Do you need to spice things up? Do you have scenes that drag? Dialogue that drones?

_____Has your manuscript been properly edited?

If you are submitting your manuscript to a traditional publisher (or an agent), has it been properly formatted? There are some universal rules, but every publisher (or agent) has their own submission guidelines. You will find a list of publishers (or agents) by doing an online search. Also, there are reference books chronicling publishers and agents. You need to pay close attention and follow these guidelines to the letter or else your manuscript will be rejected before it is even read. The biggest mistake made by new writers is submitting their proposal to the wrong person. Your manuscript is never going to be accepted if you're submitting it to a publisher (or agent) that doesn't even represent your genre. Another common mistake is sending the manuscript. Roughly 99.9 percent of publishers and agents want a proposal, *not* your manuscript. If they like what they read and think they call sell it, they will request the manuscript or at least fifty pages of it.

More about the publishing process, including how to submit your manuscript to a traditional publisher, is discussed in detail in the second book in this series, *Stop Talking & Start Publishing Your Book.*

CHAPTER TWELVE: Beta Readers and Editors

What You Need to Know About Editing

Even though you have finished writing your book, you still have work to do before you can pursue any publishing options. You need to find an editor and round up some beta readers.

Some writers don't understand the importance of editing. Your work will be full of errors if not properly edited. Even if you are a good editor, it is a bad idea to edit your own work. You may think that you don't need an editor if you're pursuing traditional publishing. Wrong! You don't want to submit a manuscript that is riddled with errors. An editor will be too focused on your errors to appreciate what you have written.

There are different types of editing services. The most common are copyediting and developmental editing so you need to figure out what you need:

Copyediting (also known as line editing or proofreading). This is usually the final editing a manuscript goes through before publishing. The editor is looking especially at rules of grammar and punctuation. The editor is not looking at your story, just at the technical components.

Developmental (also known as structural) editing. Here the editor works with the author, making suggestions on how to tighten dialogue, advice on cutting scenes, tips about character development and backstory, and constructive criticism about the story line in general. It is much more thorough than copyediting therefore it is more time-consuming and requires a greater skillset.

Since editing can be expensive, especially on longer length books and developmental/structural costs more than copyediting/line editing, you want to be sure that you're getting your money's worth. Ask the prospective editor some questions before you make any agreement. I wouldn't give an editor any money if he/she can't or won't answer these questions.

1. What types of books have you edited (fiction, nonfiction, poetry)?

2. What are your credentials? How many books have you edited? How long have you been doing this?

3. Can you give me any referrals?

4. Prior to signing a contract, can you edit one chapter or at least a few pages to make sure we'll work well together?

5. What makes you a good fit for my manuscript? What is your timeline for completing the job?

Here are some places to start to find a good editor:

Editorial Freelancers Association, www.the-efa.org

Book Editing Associates, www.book-editing.com

Writer's Digest, www.writersdigestshop.com/author-service-center

Editors' Association of Canada, http://www.editors.ca/

Society for Editors & Proofreaders UK (STEP), http://www.sfep.org.uk/

Institute for Professional Editors Australia, http://iped-editors.org/

The Book Shepherd, www.thebookshepherd.com

The Creative Penn, www.thecreativepenn.com/editors

What You Need to Know About Beta Readers...

Once you are done with edits, it is time to give your book a test run. Before you release it to the general public, you should get some feedback.

Beta readers are folks you trust to candidly and constructively read and critique your book. These should be folks who are knowledgeable about your genre and who will be honest and helpful. If you write historical fiction, don't give your book to a beta reader who only reads paranormal romance. Also, don't give your book to your best friend or your mom unless you're sure they will be honest and not just say, "Best book ever!"

Be prepared that not everyone is going to say wonderful things about your book. Don't get mad and refuse to speak to a friend just because they said they thought your book started off too slow or they didn't like one of your characters. You asked for their opinion. You want them to be honest. Sadly, writers must develop a thick skin as we are repeatedly critiqued by editors, publishers, readers, reviewers, and everyone else with an opinion.

Make sure you include a self-addressed stamped envelope and instructions for the beta reader if providing a print book. Whether you give your beta readers a PDF, e-book or print book, be sure to include a note thanking them in advance for their prompt review and provide a list of questions they should consider as they read. See Chapter Five for some questions a beta reader should be able to answer. Let them know they may ignore your suggestions. You are only providing it because some folks appreciate the guidance. Be sure to thank them again after you have received their feedback even if you don't agree with it.

I always let folks know when I expect their response as they need to know you expect them to make an effort to do this in a reasonable amount of time. Don't be disappointed if they blow the "deadline" but giving a deadline may help keep the reader on track. You may need to remind the reader but if you politely do so two or three times and there is still no response, be ready to cut your losses. I have a friend who was shocked when two of her beta readers never replied despite the fact she had asked them prior to sending the book and they had happily agreed.

Lastly, you do not have to make changes suggested by beta readers. However, if three or four folks are saying the same thing about the same scene or character, you should probably listen.

You may be wondering what you should do if you don't get good feedback from your beta readers. By this I mean they tell you "Great story!" or "I think you've got a real winner here!" This is not helpful feedback. Or maybe you're having trouble getting your beta readers to respond in a timely manner. Or you may be having trouble thinking of folks you can ask to be beta readers because you don't know anyone who reads your genre or you know they will give biased review.

In these situations you may want to check out these critique groups and resources:

www.absolutewrite.com

www.critiquecircle.com

www.internetwritingworkshop.org

www.writerscafe.com

www.writing.com

www.goodreads.com/group/show/50920-beta-reader-group

www.worldliterarycafe.com/forum/125

www.writersonlineworkshops.com/peer-critique-studio

"It's critical to hook the reader with the first page."
—John Sandford

Resources
&
Inspiration

Feng Shui or Phooey?

Sara and I discussed workspace and habits during one of our *A Writer's Journey: From Blank Page to Published* podcasts. We learned that we have very different ideas about it. I say, "Yeah, Feng Shui!" and Sara says, "Phooey!" She doesn't think it matters where you work or how you set up your workspace. She writes in a recliner using a laptop with the television full blast and her son and two dogs running around the room. She has been known to write in coffeehouses, in the car waiting outside her son's school, and all kinds of other public places.

My writing habits are completely different. I need a dedicated space and conducive work environment. To that end, I have created my ideal workspace using the principles of Feng Shui. I keep a fan beside my desk to (1) drown out all outside noise and to (2) create white noise, both of which help me to stay focused. Also, it is like the Pavlov experiment in that I have been conditioned to write when I go into my office and turn on this fan.

Your office should be a comfortable and nurturing place to write. I have all my favorite travel pictures, artwork, certificates, and memorabilia, including an exquisite wall-mounted, wood-carved elephant head from Africa, a hand-painted paddle from one of my Amazon trips, and a colorful, hand-woven rug from Morocco. Travel brings me great joy so creating this ambiance means I have created the optimum workspace for me. I am calm and creative whenever I'm in this room. I do not do other things in this space, such as eat or pay bills.

But what works for me may not work for you. Writing is not a one size fits all, so think about how to create the best writing workspace for you. I have created "A Writer's Workspace" board on my Pinterest site because I truly believe that a writer's workspace is crucial to his creativity and productivity. You can check it out, as well as my other boards on www.pinterest.com/terrancezepke.

Please be aware that you don't have to have a big space or whole room or a theme to create a good writing nook. You just have to claim the space. It's funny but Sara always swore she could write anywhere but when she had to lend her recliner to her mother who had suffered a leg injury, she discovered that she had trouble writing anywhere else. What she didn't realize is that it had become her writing space so she has come around on the whole Feng Shui concept!

I don't want to get too hung up on the whole Feng Shui philosophy. It's not really important that you know that Feng Shui is an ancient science developed more than 3,000 years ago in China or that it has to do with balancing the energy of any given space. There are three ways I think that Feng Shui can help writers, even if you don't believe in this philosophy.

1. **Clear clutter.** Throw away or remove all things that aren't necessary and relevant to your work.
2. **Get organized.** Put papers in file folders and use corkboards and cabinets. Harmonize your space.

By this I mean infuse your personality with photos, art, rugs, window treatments, furniture, etc. Get an ergonomic chair. Find a desk that works for you. I hate computer desks so I have a real wood mahogany desk that is big and solid with lots of drawers. I have it far from the door with a view to the whole room. This is not for Feng Shui, even though if practicing Feng Shui in your home or office you're supposed to put the couch or desk where you can see most of the room (for power and best energy). I did it because that's where there is a big picture window so that is the best light and place for me. You should also pay attention to colors. Your paint or wallpaper or rugs should be soft yellow or blue-green or pale gold or light blue or such. Feng Shui experts like these colors because they supposedly stimulate the mind. I like them because they make your space—whether big or tiny—light and bright, which I think is a good thing.

3. **Make your workspace a workspace only—a stress-free environment.** This means you don't use it for anything else, such as making personal calls, playing games, paying bills, or watching TV. Keep the mindset and energy in a work zone mode. As far as the stress-free environment, I'm talking about creating a calm, almost soothing space that is best for writing. Feng Shui experts recommend inserting things such as a terrarium, bamboo, or some kind of special plant, soft music

or white noise, desktop fountain or something that emits essential oils. Sara believes in the benefits of essential oils so it seems she may be abandoning her Phooey position!

Bad Feng Shui
Even if you have limited space, such as a tiny nook, claim it and use it properly. Your workspace should provide the best atmosphere or environment for writing. It should not be cluttered or used for other activities.

Good Feng Shui

I saw this image on Pinterest. An author, who had no space he could use for writing, converted a closet into an ideal workspace. Isn't this cool? **It's important to remember that every writer approaches the craft differently, from how they outline their book to their workspace. The important thing is to create the best workspace and habits for *you*.**

Best Places to Write

Got writer's block? Too many distractions? Need inspiration? Or perhaps you just need a change of environment to spark your creativity?

Here are five great places to write without distraction:

Windsor Court Hotel (New Orleans, LA) is a luxury hotel in the heart of the city. Between the hotel ambiance and the city of New Orleans, you should be well on your way to writing a bestseller!
www.windsorcourthotel.com

Wentworth Mansion (Charleston, SC) is a twenty-one-room inn that takes every guest back in time to Old Charleston. Guests will delight in the sheer luxury, from hand-carved marble fireplaces to Italian crystal chandeliers. All of this is within footsteps of historic Charleston, the inspiration and setting for hundreds of novels. The Wentworth has been voted the #1 Best Hotel in Charleston.
www.wentworthmansion.com

The Inn at Palmetto Bluff (Bluffton, SC) is located deep in the heart of the Lowcountry. If the views from this porch don't inspire you, give it up! This luxurious inn is the winner of numerous awards, including #1 Resort in the World and #1 Hotel in South Carolina. www.palmettobluff.com

Monmouth Historic Inn (Natchez, MS) is a picture-perfect antebellum plantation mansion. Built in 1818, it is now a National Historic Landmark. It offers guests the perfect retreat from the world right down to its lovely gardens and grounds. Writers need to be sure to book one of the garden cottages. You can write 'til your heart's content inside the quaint cottage or while sitting on the pretty porch overlooking the gardens. www.monmouthhistoricinn.com

Hermitage Hotel (Nashville, TN) is located in the heart of downtown Nashville, but you won't know it until you step outside. Take advantage of this ambiance to get some serious writing done or at least recharge and maybe come up with an idea for your next book or an outline. Spark your creativity with a big breakfast at the hotel's Capital Grille. You'll be ready for anything after their steak & eggs or Tennessee "Jack" egg sandwich! This AAA Five Diamond Award winning hotel has taken excellent care of its patrons since it opened its doors in 1910. www.thehermitagehotel.com

Best Writing Advice from Best-Selling Authors

"I have advice for people who want to write. I don't care whether they're 5 or 500. There are three things that are important: First if you want to write, you need to keep an honest, unpublishable journal that nobody reads, nobody but you. Where you just put down what you think about life, what you think about things, what you think is fair and what you think is unfair. And second, you need to read. You can't be a writer if you're not a reader. It's the great writers who teach us how to write. The third thing is to write. Just write a little bit every day. Even if it's for only half an hour—write, write, write."

—Madeleine L'Engle

"Start telling the stories that only you can tell because there'll always be better writers than you and there'll always be smarter writers than you. There will always be people who are much better at doing this or doing that—but you are the only you."

—Neil Gaiman

"I am always chilled and astonished by the would-be writers who ask me for advice and admit, quite blithely, that they "don't have time to read." This is like a guy starting up Mount Everest saying that he didn't have time to buy any rope or pitons."

—Stephen King

 "You either have to write or you shouldn't be writing. That's all."

—Joss Whedon

"If you want to write, if you want to create, you must be the most sublime fool that God ever turned out and sent rambling. You must write every single day of your life. You must read dreadful dumb books and glorious books, and let them wrestle in beautiful fights inside your head, vulgar one moment, brilliant the next. You must lurk in libraries and climb the stacks like ladders to sniff books like perfumes and wear books like hats upon your crazy heads. I wish you a wrestling match with your Creative Muse that will last a lifetime. I wish craziness and foolishness and madness upon you. May you live with hysteria, and out of it make fine stories— science fiction or otherwise. Which finally means, may you be in love every day for the next 20,000 days. And out of that love, remake a world."

—Ray Bradbury

"Whenever I'm asked what advice I have for young writers, I always say that the first thing is to read, and to read a lot. The second thing is to write. And the third thing, which I think is absolutely vital, is to tell stories and listen closely to the stories you're being told."

—John Green

"On writing, my advice is the same to all. If you want to be a writer, write. Write and write and write. If you stop, start again. Save everything that you write. If you feel blocked, write through it until you feel your creative juices flowing again. Write. Writing is what makes a writer, nothing more and nothing less. Ignore critics. Critics are a dime a dozen. Anybody can be a critic. Writers are priceless. Go where the pleasure is in your writing. Go where the pain is. Write the book you would like to read. Write the book you have been trying to find but have not found. But write. And remember, there are no rules for our profession. Ignore rules. Ignore what I say here if it doesn't help you. Do it your own way. Every writer knows fear and discouragement. Just write. The world is crying for new writing. It is crying for fresh and original voices and new characters and new stories. If you won't write the classics of tomorrow, well, we will not have any. Good luck."

—Anne Rice

"My first rule was given to me by TH White, author of *The Sword in the Stone* and other Arthurian fantasies and was: read. Read everything you can lay hands on. I always advise people who want to write a fantasy or science fiction or romance to stop reading everything in those genres and start reading everything else from Bunyan to Byatt."

—Michael Moorcock

"What I did have, which others perhaps didn't, was a capacity for sticking at it, which really is the point, not the talent at all. You have to stick at it."

—Doris Lessing

"You can't wait for inspiration. You have to go after it with a club."

—Jack London

"Stay hungry; the more you want it, the more likely you'll become a writer. You must want to enough. Enough to take all the rejections, enough to pay the price in disappointment and discouragement while you are learning. Like any other artist you must learn your craft—then you can add all the genius you like."

—Phyllis Whitney

"Remember that you're not alone—even famous authors struggle to become writers. Every writer I know has trouble writing."

—Joseph Heller

"Don't expect writing to be easy. Writing a book is a horrible, exhausting struggle, like a long bout of some painful illness. One would never undertake such a thing if one were not driven on by some demon whom one can neither resist nor understand."

—George Orwell

"If writing seems hard, it's because it is hard. It's one of the hardest things people do."

—William Zinsser

"Advice to young writers? Always the same advice: learn to trust our own judgment, learn inner independence, learn to trust that time will sort the good from the bad—including your own bad."

—Doris Lessing

"Write. Start writing today. Start writing right now. Don't write it right, just write it—and then make it right later. Give yourself the mental freedom to enjoy the process, because the process of writing is a long one. Be wary of 'writing rules' and advice. Do it your way."

—Tara Moss

Weird Writing Rituals of Famous Writers

Maya Angelou left her apartment every morning at 7:00 a.m. to go to a hotel room where she wrote until 2:00 p.m. She always brought a bottle of sherry, a deck of cards, and her Bible with her.

Honoré de Balzac ate a light dinner and retired to bed by 6:00 p.m. He awoke at 1:00 a.m. and wrote until 8:00 a.m. He took an hour and a half nap and then wrote until 4:00 p.m. He then took a walk, visited with friends, took a bath, and went to bed by 6:00 pm. As if doing this routine was not remarkable enough, he consumed fifty cups of coffee daily!

**Ernest Hemingway** usually wrote standing up. He grabbed pages out of his typewriter and threw them onto the floor when he felt

his writing was unacceptable. He always stopped writing while he still had something to say so that he had a good starting point the next day.

Truman Capote wrote while lying down and while drinking coffee and chain-smoking cigarettes. As the day progressed, he transitioned from coffee to mint tea to sherry to martinis.

Dan Brown often hangs upside down in antigravity books for inspiration. He keeps an hourglass on his desk and does exercise and stretching every hour on the hour.

Best Writing Blogs and Podcasts

Judith Briles, www.authoru.org

K. M. Weiland, www.helpingwritersbecomeauthors.com

Terrance Zepke (*A Writer's Journey: From Blank Page to Published*) www.terrancezepke.com/category/podcasts/a-writers-journey

Sara Whitford (*A Writer's Journey: From Blank Page to Published*) www.sarawhitford.com

Jane Friedman, janefriedman.com/blog/

Jeff Goins, www.goinswriter.com

Joel Friedlander, www.thebookdesigner.com

Nina Amir, ninaamir.com

Victoria Mixon, www.victoriamixon.com

Anne R Allen, www.anneallen.blogspot.com

Debbie Ridpath Ohi, www.inkygirl.com

Frances Caballo,
www.facebook.com/SocialMediaJustforWriters?pnref=l
hc

Jason Matthews, ebooksuccess4free.wordpress.com/

For more writing blogs check out
positivewriter.com/best-writing-blogs/

Ten Writing Exercises

Writing gets better with practice. Even gifted writers need writing experience to improve their craft. Here are some ways you can improve your writing and finish your book:

1. Rewrite a classic fairy tale. This is a great creative writing exercise.

2. Write a pitch letter to an agent or publisher.

3. Write your book's title and description.

4. Rewrite one important description in your book.

5. Write a short story using five random words from the dictionary.

6. Write a short story using the first page of a book you know well, preferably one in the same genre. Only use the first few paragraphs of that story to get you started. The rest, including your ending, should be very different.

7. Rewrite a scene from your story using a different point of view. Was the scene better or worse with this revision?

8. Rewrite a key scene with your protagonist giving him/her three different traits. How did this affect your story?

9. Rewrite your ending to be completely different. Is it now better or worse?

10. Add another character and/or complication to your story. Again, ask yourself if this helped or hindered your story.

BONUS!

MONTH-BY-MONTH GUIDE TO WRITING A BOOK

Month #1: Write A Book

This step-by-step (or rather month-by-month) approach is meant to be used in conjunction with the information found throughout this book. So let's start at the beginning. Why have you been talking so long about writing a book but done nothing about it? What's your excuse? Seriously? Take five minutes and sit down and make a list. What's on your list? Don't know how to get started? Lack of time? Lack of talent? Lack of knowledge? Fear? I can help you with everything but the talent part. But if you have what it takes, I can show you how to make your dream a reality.

The hardest part is getting started. I've been doing this a long time, and I can tell you that you can buy all the writing books you can afford, subscribe to the best writers' blogs, and attend conferences until *you* could teach writing workshops, but if you don't "get butt in chair" you won't get there. It can be daunting to stare at a big, blank computer screen. But the good news is almost nothing is impossible in this world and this day and age. So, if you'll make the resolution, I will see to it that you achieve your goal.

ASSIGNMENT Month #1: Write down your IDEA. I hate to say it but if you don't even have a single idea for a book, you may not be a writer. But if you have an idea, you need to turn that idea into a manuscript. How? First, you need to summarize that idea in a minimum of one sentence and a maximum of five sentences. This is non-negotiable! You must be able to sum up your story. This month's assignment is to work on defining and summarizing your idea. I found these examples for a well-known story, *The Hobbit,* on www.imdb.com/title/tt0903624/plotsummary. I recommend a maximum of a three-sentence summary.

Example #1: An inexperienced hobbit inherits a magic ring and must journey to a faraway land to destroy it.

Example #2: Bilbo Baggins is swept into a quest to reclaim the lost Dwarf Kingdom of Erebor from the fearsome dragon Smaug. Approached out of the blue by the wizard Gandalf the Grey, Bilbo finds himself joining a company of thirteen dwarves led by the legendary warrior, Thorin Oakenshield. Their journey will take them into the Wild, through treacherous lands swarming with goblins and orcs, deadly wargs and giant spiders, shapeshifters and sorcerers. Although their goal lies to the East and the wastelands of the

Lonely Mountain, first they must escape the goblin tunnels, where Bilbo meets the creature that will change his life forever…Gollum. Here, alone with Gollum, on the shores of an underground lake, the unassuming Bilbo Baggins not only discovers depths of guile and courage that surprise even him, he also gains possession of Gollum's "precious" ring that holds unexpected and useful qualities. A simple, gold ring that is tied to the fate of all Middle-Earth in ways Bilbo cannot begin to know.

Example #3: Once upon a time, the Kingdom of Erebor in the Lonely Mountain was taken from the dwarfs by the evil dragon Smaug. One day, the young hobbit Bilbo Baggins is unexpectedly visited by the wizard Gandalf the Grey and twelve homeless dwarfs led by their former king, Thorin. Bilbo joins the company in an unexpected journey through dangerous lands of the Middle-Earth where they have to fight against trolls, orcs, and other creatures. Bilbo also meets Gollum and finds a magic ring that is the key to everything.

Example #4: A reluctant hobbit, Bilbo Baggins, sets out to the Lonely Mountain with a spirited group of dwarves to reclaim their mountain home—and the gold within it—from the dragon Smaug.

Month #2: Write A Book

If you're reading this, I hope this means that you have completed the first month's assignment. During the first month, I asked you to (1) identify what's holding you back and let it go and (2) to take the first step: Write Down Your Idea. So, now that you have your story summary done, it is time to move on to your second assignment.

ASSIGNMENT Month #2: Outline your novel.
Before you build a house, you must put down the foundation. This is a critical step in the process, so it should not be skipped in your enthusiasm to get writing. By taking the time to do this step now, you will have a roadmap in hand to follow so that you won't detour off a cliff like Wild Coyote! I have discussed all the ways you can outline your book in Chapter One.

Month #3: Write A Book

This month is all about word count and characters. Let's start with your word count. The goal is a 70,000-word novel. This is the average novel length with some being about 60,000 words and others somewhere in the 80,000–90,000 word range. To achieve this goal, you need ten months to write:

10,000 words each month, which is 2,500 words a week or 500 words a day with two days off a week

As you're writing towards this month's goal, be sure to map out your cast of characters. Have you figured out your cast of characters? Who's your protagonist? Who else will be in your story? Most novels are character-driven, so you need to give serious consideration as to your protagonist and what you want, need, and expect from physical traits to personality traits.

ASSIGNMENT Month #3: Write 10,000 words. Do not edit at this point. Just keep writing. Editing will come later. Also, use whatever method you like, such as index cards or Excel spreadsheet, to create "maps" of all of your characters. This will not only help you keep things straight as you progress and introduce more characters, but this will also help you discover and define your characters. Refer to Chapter Four to determine your point of view. You have to know who's telling your story before you can tell it.

Month #4: Write A Book

ASSIGNMENT Month #4: Write another 10,000 words. As you are going forward, be sure you are addressing all the elements required to create a good novel. Review Chapter Four and make sure you're getting it right.

Month #5: Write A Book

Deal with distractions. Figure out what is getting in your way and then fix it. Maybe you're trying to write at a time that won't work because your kids are home from school. Maybe you're not allowing enough time or maybe you're trying to write at a time that is not best for you creatively. Take a few minutes and think about what your biggest problem is and what you can do to improve the situation. Refer to Chapter Eight for more ways to deal with distractions.

ASSIGNMENT Month #5: Write another 10,000 words. Stay focused and on track. Inevitably, there will be some who want to pick up the pace. You may be tempted to skip or skim or somehow shortcut the process. While I admire your enthusiasm, I urge you to stay the course. If you jump the gun, you may end up having to rewrite most of your draft because haste makes waste. In your rush to write more, you wrote a lot, but they weren't the right words. You forgot about essential elements of a breakout novel.

Month #6: Write A Book

Now is the time to ask yourself the tough questions.

Q. *Is this plot realistic but not obvious?* (**PLAUSIBILITY**)

Q. *What is the conflict?* (**CONFLICT**)

Q. *What makes your story unique?* (**ORIGINALITY**)

Q. *What kind of response are you expecting from readers?* (**GUT EMOTIONAL APPEAL**)

*Refer to Chapter Nine for more about the three P's and three C's.

ASSIGNMENT Month #6: Write another 10,000 words.

Month #7: Write A Book

Get help if you need it. Join a writers group or writing challenge or attend a writers-in-residence program. Refer to Chapter Two for resources.

ASSIGNMENT Month #7: Write another 10,000 words.

Month #8: Write A Book

Pat yourself on the back! You have written 50,000 words or more at this point. Can you believe it? Now stay the course. Don't let yourself get derailed. Review Chapters Eight and Ten. If you're struggling, don't sweat it. Put the manuscript aside for a couple of days and then come back to it refreshed and ready to write.

ASSIGNMENT Month #8: Write another 10,000 words.

Month #9: Write A Book

If you're still struggling as to how to proceed with your story GET HELP AND GET OVER IT! See Chapter Ten for resources for handling this common problem. Join a group or a writing challenge or simply make yourself sit down and write something. Try a writing exercise to jump-start things. Once you start, you will find your way back, I promise.

ASSIGNMENT Month #9: Write another 10,000 words.

Month #10: Write A Book

ASSIGNMENT Month #10: Write another 10,000 words or whatever is necessary if you're not done yet. Read the last 50 pages of your manuscript and give it a critical review to make sure it passes muster. Refer to Chapter Eleven for a Manuscript Checklist.

Month #11: Write A Book

By this point, you should be done writing your first draft. Now you need to do some editing. Refer to Chapter Twelve about what kind of editing you need to do and where to find help.

Assignment Month #11: Edit your manuscript.

Month #12: Write A Book

Now you are ready to send your beloved manuscript out to some beta readers. No argument. No excuses. The time has come. You need to get some objective feedback about what you have written.

Assignment Month #12: Send your manuscript to at least three beta readers. See Chapter Twelve for more on this process. After you have received your feedback, you can begin working on your second draft. This may or may not be your final draft. Keep writing and editing until you get there. When you are ready to publish, check out *Stop Talking and Start Publishing Your Book* for a step-by-step tutorial on how to proceed.

Titles by Terrance

www.terrancezepke.com

www.terrancetalkstravel.com

Travel Guidebooks:

The Encyclopedia of Cheap Travel: Save Up to 90% on Lodging, Flight, Tours, Cruises and More! (Lookout Publishing)

Spookiest Lighthouses: Discover America's Most Haunted Lighthouses (Safari Publishing)

Spookiest Battlefields: Discover America's Most Haunted Battlefields (Safari Publishing)

Terrance Talks Travel: A Pocket Guide to African Safaris (Safari Publishing)

Terrance Talks Travel: A Pocket Guide to Adventure Travel (Safari Publishing)

 *Terrance Talks Travel: A Pocket Guide to South Africa* (Safari Publishing)

Coastal North Carolina: Its Enchanting Islands, Towns, and Communities (Pineapple Press)

Coastal South Carolina: Welcome to the Lowcountry (Pineapple Press)

Lighthouses of the Carolinas (Pineapple Press)

A Ghost Hunter's Guide to The Most Haunted Hotels & Inns in America (Safari Publishing)

A Ghost Hunter's Guide to The Most Haunted Places in America (Safari Publishing)

A Ghost Hunter's Guide to The Most Haunted Houses in America (Safari Publishing)

Ghost Books:

The Best Ghost Tales of South Carolina (Pineapple Press)

Ghosts of the Carolina Coasts (Pineapple Press)

Ghosts and Legends of the Carolina Coasts (Pineapple Press)

The Best Ghost Tales of North Carolina (Pineapple Press)

Ghosts of Savannah (Pineapple Press)

Special Interest Titles:

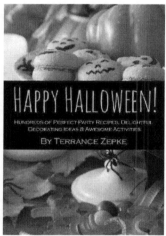 *Happy Halloween! Hundreds of Perfect Party Recipes, Delightful Decorating Ideas & Awesome Activities* (Safari Publishing)

Pirates of the Carolinas (Pineapple Press)

Stop Talking & Start Writing Your Book! (Safari Publishing)

Stop Talking & Start Publishing Your Book! (Safari Publishing)

Stop Talking & Start Selling Your Book! (Safari Publishing)

*Lowcountry Voodoo: Tales, Spells and Boo Hags* (Pineapple Press)

Books for Kids (8–12 years old)

Ghosts of the Carolinas for Kids (Pineapple Press)

Pirates of the Carolinas for Kids (Pineapple Press)

Lighthouses of the Carolinas for Kids (Pineapple Press)

*Fiction titles are written under a pseudonym

Index

Dear Reader,

Thank you for buying or borrowing **_Stop Talking & Start Writing Your Book._** I hope you enjoyed it—and learned a lot!

I spent a great deal of time compiling this information into what I believe is an easy-to-read, useful reference. I would love to hear from you if you'd like to post a comment on www.terrancezepke.com. I do respond to all comments. If you'd like to learn more about writing, publishing, and selling your book be sure to sign up for my _A Writer's Journey_ blog.

I would also like to ask you to please share your feedback about this book on Amazon and/or Goodreads so that other readers might discover this title too.

Authors appreciate readers more than you realize and we dearly love and depend upon good reviews! If you've never posted a review before it is easy to do…just tell folks what you liked or didn't like about this book and why you (hopefully) recommend it. http://www.amazon.com/Terrance-Zepke/e/B000APJNIA/

Thank you again for your interest and best of luck in your future writing endeavors…

Terrance

Notes

Terrance Zepke